A Young Vic/Royal Court The[...]
co-production with Birming[...]
Repertory Theatre, Sheffiel[...]
and The Yard Theatre

Cuttin' It

by Charlene James

Cuttin' It is part of the Royal Court's Jerwood New
Playwrights Programme, supported by the Jerwood
Charitable Foundation.

Cuttin' It was first performed at the Young Vic on Friday 20 May 2016
and at the Royal Court Jerwood Theatre Upstairs, Sloane Square, on
Thursday 23 June 2016.

Cuttin' It
by Charlene James

CAST (in alphabetical order)

Muna **Adelayo Adedayo**
Iqra **Tsion Habte**

Direction **Gbolahan Obisesan**
Design **Joanna Scotcher**
Light **Azusa Ono**
Sound **Adrienne Quartly**
Casting **Amy Ball**
Voice **Hazel Holder**
Assistant Director **Anastasia Osei-Kuffour***
Design Assistant **Daisy Young**

Company Stage Manager/Touring Production Manager **Nick Hill**
Deputy Stage Manager **Mica Taylor**
Costume Supervisor **Rosey Morling**
Touring Relighter/Production Electrician **Costa Cambanakis**
Touring Production Carpenter **Hilary Williamson**
Lighting Operator (Young Vic) **Nell Allen**
Lighting Operator (Royal Court) **Matt Harding**
Wardrobe Maintenance **Nicki Martin-Harper**
Set Built By **Young Vic Workshops**
Scenic Artist **Natasha Shepherd**

With generous support from the Richenthal Foundation

Cuttin' It is supported by the Genesis Foundation.

*Anastasia Osei-Kuffour is supported through the Jerwood Assistant Directors Program at the Young Vic.

Cuttin' It
by Charlene James

Charlene James (Writer)

Awards include: **BBC Audio Drama Award for Best Single Drama, Alfred Fagon Award, George Devine Award (Cuttin' It).**

Charlene is a playwright and actor who trained at Birmingham School of Acting and The School at Steppenwolf, Chicago. In 2008, she participated in the Royal Court's Young Writers Programme and in 2012 she was selected to be one of the 503 Five at Theatre 503. In 2013 Charlene became a writer in residence at the Birmingham Rep and wrote Jump! We'll Catch You for their season focusing on mental health. Her play, Tweet Tweet, was commissioned by the Birmingham Rep as part of Young Theatre Makers and premiered there before touring.

Adelayo Adedayo (Muna)

Theatre includes: **Klippies (Southwark Playhouse); Rachel (Finborough); The Dead Wait (Park).**

Television includes: **Black to the Future, Houdini & Doyle, Stan Lee's Lucky Man, Law & Order UK, Some Girls, Skins, Meet the Bandalis.**

Film includes: **Unlocked, Jet Trash, London Fields, Gone Too Far, Sket.**

Tsion Habte (Iqra)

Tsion is making her professional stage debut in Cuttin' It.

Hazel Holder (Voice)

As Performer, for the Young Vic: **The Sleeping Beauty (& Barbican/Broadway).**

As Performer, other theatre includes: **Here We Go, As You Like It (choir), Medea, Death & the King's Horseman (National); The Bakkhai (Almeida); The Tempest (RSC); Journey to Freedom (Marginal Voices); Dart's Love (Tête-à-Tête Opera Festival); Zero (Clod Ensemble); Cave of Wonders, Tamba Tamba (Tiata Fahodzi); White Suit, Dalston Songs (& ROH), Songs of Exile (& ROH) (Helen Chadwick Song Theatre); The Bacchae (Royal Exchange, Manchester); Six Characters in Search of an Author (Headlong); The Bacchae (National Theatre of Scotland/Broadway); Fingerprint (ROH2); Critical Mass, Lip (The Shout); Myths & Hymns (Finborough); Mercy Fine (Clean Break); Trojan Women – Women of Owu (Collective Artistes); Mourning Song (Black Mime); Maskarade (Talawa); Carmen Jones, Ain't Misbehavin' (West End).**

TV includes: **EastEnders, Judge John Deed, Doctors, The Cambridge Spies, The Bill.**

Film includes: **The Followed, Dates.**

Radio includes: **Something Understood, Death & the King's Horseman, The Ern & Vern Show, Roots, Solomon Child, Telephone in the Deep Freeze.**

As Voice & Dialect Coach, theatre includes: **Les Blancs, Ma Rainey's Black Bottom (National); The Rolling Stone (Orange Tree/Royal Exchange, Manchester); F*ck The Polar Bears (Bush); Misanthropes (Old Vic New Voices Festival); Eclipsed, The Rise & Shine of Comrade Fiasco (Gate); The Initiate (Paines Plough); The Epic Adventure of Nhamo (Tiata Fahodzi).**

Hazel teaches as a Voice & Dialect Coach at Arts Ed, RADA, ALRA, Royal Central School of Speech & Drama and Guildhall School of Music & Drama. Hazel also works with Marginal Voices, a charity that helps trafficked women dramatise their experiences.

Gbolahan Obisesan (Direction)

As Director, for the Young Vic: **Sus.**

As Director, for the Royal Court: **School Gate (The Guardian Microplay).**

As Co-Writer, for the Young Vic & Royal Court: **Feast.**

As Writer, for the Young Vic: **Mad About The Boy.**

As Director, other theatre includes: **We Are Proud to Present..., Sixty-Six Books (Bush); Songs Inside (Gate); Eye/Balls, Hold It Up (Soho) 200 Years (Watford Palace).**

As Associate Director, theatre includes: **The Comedy of Errors, FELA! (National); Julius Caesar (RSC); Magic Flute (West End).**

As Writer, other theatre includes: **Pigeon English (Bristol Old Vic/Edinburgh Fringe Festival); Set Me Fair (Latitude); Sweet Mother, Regeneration, A Vision of Pride (503); Deconstructing the Barack (Tristan Bates); Hold it up (Soho).**

Awards include: **The Scotsman Fringe First Award for Best Play (Mad About The Boy); Jerwood Directors Award (Sus).**

Azusa Ono (Light)

Theatre includes: **I Know All The Secrets In My World (Tiata Fahodzi/Tour); Dot, Squiggle & Rest (Polka Theatre/ROH); Peddling (HighTide Festival/New York 59E59/Tour); We Are Proud to Present... (Bush); Copyright Christmas (Barbican); Fanfared by Invisible Flock (Crucible, Sheffield); Choreogata (Southbank Centre).**

Azusa has been creating lighting design for various types of shows since she studied fine arts in Japan and trained in lighting design at the RCSSD in London.

Anastasia Osei-Kuffour (Assistant Director)

As Director, for the Young Vic: **For the All The Ways to Say Goodbye, Fresh Direction Project.**

As Assistant Director, for the Royal Court: **Plaques & Tangles.**

As Director, theatre includes: **Here Comes The Bride, Black Lives, Black Words (Bush); Interregnum (Rose); Hosea's Girl (Talawa Firsts); You Know That I'll Be Back, Universally Speaking (503); Pushers (Etcetera).**

As Assistant Director, other theatre includes: **Three Generations of Women (Greenwich); Alpha Beta (Finborough); Henry V (Unicorn); Idomeneus (Gate).**

As Associate Director, theatre includes: **Flowering Cherry (Finborough); Hackney Volpone (The Rose Lipman Building).**

As Boris Karloff Trainee Assistant Director, theatre includes: **A Doll's House (Young Vic).**

Anastasia trained as a director through the Young Vic Directors Programme. She is currently Creative Associate at the Gate Theatre, and has recently finished as resident assistant director at the Finborough Theatre. As artistic director of Wrested Veil Theatre Company she received the Talawa studio firsts award for developing a new dance theatre play Hosea's Girl.

JERWOOD CHARITABLE FOUNDATION

Adrienne Quartly (Sound)

As Sound Designer, for the Young Vic: **The Container, The Shawl.**

As Sound Designer, for the Royal Court: **93.2fm.**

As Sound Designer, other theatre Includes: **Opening Skinner's Box (Improbable); I Am Thomas (National Theatre of Scotland); Bad Jews (Theatre Royal Haymarket); Splendour (Donmar); The Whipping Man, Merit (Plymouth Theatre Royal); The Ghost Train, Too Clever by Half, You Can't Take It With You (Royal Exchange, Manchester); Get Happy (Barbican); Here Lies Mary Spindler (RSC); The Ladykillers (Newbury Watermill); After Electra (Tricycle); Sex & The Three Day Week (Liverpool Everyman); Grand Guignol (Southwark Playhouse/Drum, Plymouth); Untold Stories (West Yorkshire Playhouse); Every Last Trick (Spymonkey); Tale of Two Cities, My Zinc Bed, Private Fears in Public Places, Just Between Ourselves, Habeas Corpus, Quartermaine's Terms (Royal & Derngate, Northampton); Inside Wagner's Head (Linbury, ROH); Fräuline Julie (after August Strindberg) (Barbican/Schaubühne); Rings of Saturn (halle kalk, Cologne); Body of an American, Tejas Verdes (Gate); Stockholm (frantic assembly); 365 (National Theatre of Scotland); The Roundabout Season (Paines Plough); And The Horse You Rode In On (Barbican Bite Festival); 4000 miles (Theatre Royal, Bath); The Fastest Clock in the Universe (Hampstead); Woyzeck (St. Ann's Warehouse, New York); The Importance of Being Earnest (Rose, Kingston/Hong Kong Festival); The Vortex (Rose, Kingston); One Monkey Don't Stop No Show, A Raisin in the Sun (Eclipse); Chekhov In Hell, The Astronaut's Chair, Nostalgia (Drum, Plymouth).**

As Sound Designer & Composer, theatre includes: **I'd Rather Goya Robbed Me of My Sleep than Some Other Arsehole (Gate); The Tragedy of Thomas Hobbes (RSC).**

As Composer, theatre includes: **The Whipping Man (Drum, Plymouth); Faustus, The School for Scandal, Volpone, The Duchess of Malfi (stage on screen/Greenwich); Rumpelstiltskin (Norwich Puppet Theatre); Three Little Pigs, The Balloon Gardener, Lighter Than Air (circo ridiculoso); Dream Story (Gate); A Christmas Carol (Sherman Cymru); The Painter, Enemy of the People (Arcola).**

Joanna Scotcher (Design)

For the Young Vic: **A Harlem Dream.**

For the Royal Court: **Pests, The Caravan (& Look Left Look Right).**

Other theatre includes: **The Rolling Stone, Anna Karenina (Royal Exchange, Manchester/West Yorkshire Playhouse); The Railway Children (York Theatre Royal/Waterloo Station/Kings Cross Station); Antigone (Pilot); Arabian Nights (Birmingham Rep/Coney); Hopelessly Devoted (Paines Plough); Billy The Girl (Soho/ Clean Break); Silly Kings (National Theatre Wales); Above & Beyond (Look Left Look Right); Marvellous Imaginary Menagerie (Les Enfants Terribles); House Of Cards (Kensington Palace/ Coney); Platform (Old Vic Tunnels); All That Is Solid Melts Into Air (Tangled Feet/Greenwich International Festival/National); Young Pretender (Nabakov); Counted (Roundhouse/ Look Left Look Right/West Yorkshire Playhouse); Inches Apart (Old Vic New Voices).**

Awards include: **WhatsOnStage Award for Best Set Designer (The Railway Children).**

The Railway Children went on to win the Olivier Award for Best Entertainment. As well as her theatrical stage design, Joanna specialises in the world of immersive performance and site responsive design, inhabiting spaces from the intimate to the epic. Her design work has been exhibited at the V&A and her installations have appeared at Kensington Palace and Covent Garden. Joanna recently designed the Capturing the Flame Ceremony for the inaugural European Games in Baku, Azerbaijan. Joanna forms part of the multi-award-winning theatre company LookLeftLookRight as associate designer.

JERWOOD CHARITABLE FOUNDATION

Jerwood New Playwrights is a longstanding partnership between Jerwood Charitable Foundation and the Royal Court. Each year, Jerwood New Playwrights supports the production of three new works by emerging writers, all of whom are in the first 10 years of their career.

The Royal Court carefully identifies playwrights whose careers would benefit from the challenge and profile of being fully produced either in the Jerwood Downstairs or Jerwood Upstairs Theatres at the Royal Court.

Since 1994, the programme has produced a collection of challenging and outspoken works which explore a variety of new forms and voices and so far has supported the production of 82 new plays. These plays include: Joe Penhall's **Some Voices**, Nick Grosso's **Peaches** and **Real Classy Affair**, Judy Upton's **Ashes and Sand**, Sarah Kane's **Blasted, Cleansed** and **4.48 Psychosis**, Michael Wynne's **The Knocky** and **The People are Friendly**, Judith Johnson's **Uganda**, Sebastian Barry's **The Steward of Christendom**, Jez Butterworth's **Mojo**, Mark Ravenhill's **Shopping and Fucking**, Ayub Khan Din's **East is East** and **Notes on Falling Leaves**, Martin McDonagh's **The Beauty Queen of Leenane**, Jess Walters' **Cockroach, Who?**, Tamantha Hammerschlag's **Backpay**, Connor McPherson's **The Weir**, Meredith Oakes' **Faith**, Rebecca Prichard's **Fair Game**, Roy Williams' **Lift Off, Clubland** and **Fallout**, Richard Bean's **Toast** and **Under the Whaleback**, Gary Mitchell's **Trust** and **The Force of Change**, Mick Mahoney's **Sacred Heart** and **Food Chain**, Marina Carr's **On Raftery's Hill**, David Eldridge's **Under the Blue Sky** and **Incomplete and Random Acts of Kindness**, David Harrower's **Presence**, Simon Stephens' **Herons, Country Music**

and **Motortown**, Leo Butler's **Redundant** and **Lucky Dog**, Enda Walsh's **Bedbound**, David Greig's **Outlying Islands**, Zinnie Harris' **Nightingale and Chase**, Grae Cleugh's **Fucking Games**, Rona Munro's **Iron**, Ché Walker's **Fleshwound**, Laura Wade's **Breathing Corpses**, debbie tucker green's **Stoning Mary**, Gregory Burke's **On Tour**, Stella Feehily's **O Go My Man**, Simon Faquhar's **Rainbow Kiss**, April de Angelis, Stella Feehily, Tanika Gupta, Chloe Moss and Laura Wade's **Catch**, Polly Stenham's **That Face** and **Tusk Tusk**, Mike Bartlett's **My Child**, Fiona Evans' **Scarborough**, Levi David Addai's **Oxford Street**, Bola Agbaje's **Gone Too Far!** and **Off The Endz**, Alexi Kaye Campbell's **The Pride**, Alia Bano's **Shades**, Tim Crouch's **The Author**, DC Moore's **The Empire**, Anya Reiss' **Spur of the Moment** and **The Acid Test**, Penelope Skinner's **The Village Bike**, Rachel De-lahay's **The Westbridge** and **Routes**, Nick Payne's **Constellations**, Vivienne Franzmann's **The Witness** and **Pests**, E. V. Crowe's **Hero**, Anders Lustgarten's **If You Don't Let Us Dream, We Won't Let You Sleep**, Suhayla El-Bushra's **Pigeons**, Clare Lizzimore's **Mint**, Alistair McDowall's **Talk Show**, Rory Mullarkey's **The Wolf From The Door**, Molly Davies' **God Bless The Child**, Diana Nneka Atuona's **Liberian Girl**, Cordelia Lynn's **Lela & Co.** and Stef Smith's **Human Animals**.

Jerwood Charitable Foundation is dedicated to imaginative and responsible revenue funding of the arts, supporting artists to develop and grow at important stages in their careers. It works with artists across art forms, from dance and theatre to literature, music and the visual arts.

jerwoodcharitablefoundation.org

CUTTIN' IT UK TOUR

A Young Vic/Royal Court co-production with Birmingham Repertory Theatre, Sheffield Theatres and The Yard Theatre.

20 May–11 June
Young Vic Theatre
66 The Cut, London SE1 8LZ
www.youngvic.org

14–18 June
Birmingham Repertory Theatre
Centenary Square, Broad Street, Birmingham, B1 2EP
www.birmingham-rep.co.uk

23 June–13 July
Royal Court Theatre
Sloane Square, London, SW1W 8AS
www.royalcourttheatre.com

15 July
Latitude Festival
Henham Park
www.latitudefestival.com

20–23 July
Sheffield Crucible Studio
55 Norfolk Street, Sheffield, S1 1DA
www.sheffieldtheatres.co.uk

26–30 July
The Yard Theatre
Unit 2a Queen's Yard, London, E9 5EN
www.theyardtheatre.co.uk

Cuttin' It is part of the A Nation's Theatre Festival
www.anationsheatre.org.uk

THE ROYAL COURT THEATRE

The Royal Court Theatre is the writers' theatre. It is the leading force in world theatre for energetically cultivating writers – undiscovered, emerging and established.

Through the writers, the Royal Court is at the forefront of creating restless, alert, provocative theatre about now. We open our doors to the unheard voices and free thinkers that, through their writing, change our way of seeing.

Over 120,000 people visit the Royal Court in Sloane Square, London, each year and many thousands more see our work elsewhere through transfers to the West End and New York, UK and international tours, digital platforms, our residencies across London, and our site-specific work. Through all our work we strive to inspire audiences and influence future writers with radical thinking and provocative discussion.

The Royal Court's extensive development activity encompasses a diverse range of writers and artists and includes an ongoing programme of writers' attachments, readings, workshops and playwriting groups. Twenty years of the International Department's pioneering work around the world means the Royal Court has relationships with writers on every continent.

Within the past sixty years, John Osborne, Samuel Beckett, Arnold Wesker, Ann Jellicoe, Howard Brenton, David Hare and many more started their careers at the Court.

Many others, including Caryl Churchill, Athol Fugard, Mark Ravenhill, Simon Stephens, debbie tucker green and Sarah Kane have followed.

More recently, the theatre has fostered new writers such as Lucy Kirkwood, Nick Payne, Penelope Skinner and Alistair McDowall and produced many iconic plays from Laura Wade's **Posh** to Jez Butterworth's **Jerusalem** and Martin McDonagh's **Hangmen.**

Royal Court plays from every decade are now performed on stage and taught in classrooms and universities across the globe.

It is because of this commitment to the writer that we believe there is no more important theatre in the world than the Royal Court.

Supported using public funding by
**ARTS COUNCIL
ENGLAND**

ROYAL

IN 2016 THE ROYAL COURT IS 60 YEARS NEW

17 May – 21 May
Ophelias Zimmer
Directed by Katie Mitchell
Designed by Chloe Lamford
Text by Alice Birch
In association with Schaubühne Berlin

2 Jun – 11 Jun
MINEFIELD (LIFT 2016)
By Lola Arias
A Royal Court Theatre co-commission with
LIFT, Brighton Festival, Le Quai Angers
and Künstlerhaus Mousonturm. Produced by
LIFT. A House on Fire project, supported by
the Culture Programme of the European Union.

1 Jul – 6 Aug
Unreachable
By Anthony Neilson

7 Sep – 15 Oct
Torn
By Nathaniel Martello-White

15 Sep – 22 Oct
Father Comes Home From The Wars (Parts 1, 2 & 3)
By Suzan-Lori Parks

Tickets from £10. 020 7565 5000 (no booking fee)
royalcourttheatre.com

ROYAL COURT SUPPORTERS

The Royal Court is a registered charity and not-for-profit company. We need to raise £1.7 million every year in addition to our core grant from the Arts Council and our ticket income to achieve what we do.

We have significant and longstanding relationships with many generous organisations and individuals who provide vital support. Royal Court supporters enable us to remain the writers' theatre, find stories from everywhere and create theatre for everyone.

We can't do it without you.

Coutts supports Innovation at the Royal Court. The Genesis Foundation supports the Royal Court's work with International Playwrights. Bloomberg supports Beyond the Court. Jerwood Charitable Foundation supports emerging writers through the Jerwood New Playwrights series. The Pinter Commission is given annually by his widow, Lady Antonia Fraser, to support a new commission at the Royal Court.

PUBLIC FUNDING

Arts Council England, London
British Council

CHARITABLE DONATIONS

The Austin & Hope
   Pilkington Trust
Martin Bowley Charitable Trust
The City Bridge Trust
The Clifford Chance
   Foundation
Cockayne - Grants for the Arts
The Ernest Cook Trust
Cowley Charitable Trust
The Dorset Foundation
The Eranda Foundation
Lady Antonia Fraser for
   The Pinter Commission
Genesis Foundation
The Golden Bottle Trust

The Haberdashers' Company
Roderick & Elizabeth Jack
Jerwood Charitable
   Foundation
Kirsh Foundation
The Mackintosh Foundation
Marina Kleinwort Trust
The Andrew Lloyd Webber
   Foundation
The London Community
   Foundation
John Lyon's Charity
Clare McIntyre's Bursary
The Andrew W. Mellon
   Foundation
The Mercers' Company
The Portrack Charitable Trust
The David & Elaine Potter
   Foundation
The Richard Radcliffe
   Charitable Trust
Rose Foundation
Royal Victoria Hall Foundation
The Sackler Trust
The Sobell Foundation
John Thaw Foundation
The Vandervoll Foundation
Sir Siegmund Warburg's
   Voluntary Settlement
The Garfield Weston
   Foundation
The Wolfson Foundation

CORPORATE SPONSORS

AKA
AlixPartners
Aqua Financial Solutions Ltd
Bloomberg
Colbert
Coutts
Edwardian Hotels, London
Fever-Tree
Gedye & Sons

Kudos
MAC
Nyetimber

BUSINESS MEMBERS

Auerbach & Steele
   Opticians
CNC – Communications &
   Network Consulting
Cream
Hugo Boss UK
Lansons
Left Bank Pictures
Rockspring Property
   Investment Managers
Tetragon Financial Group
Vanity Fair

DEVELOPMENT COUNCIL

Majella Altschuler
Piers Butler
Sarah Chappatte
Cas Donald
Celeste Fenichel
Piers Gibson
Emma Marsh
Angelie Moledina
Anatol Orient
Andrew Rodger
Deborah Shaw
Sian Westerman

Remember the Royal Court in your will and help to ensure that our future is as iconic as our past.

Every gift, whatever the amount, will help us maintain and care for the building, support the next generation of playwrights starting out in their career, deliver our education programme and put our plays on the stage.

LEAVE A LEGACY

To discuss leaving a legacy to the Royal Court, please contact:

Liv Nilssen, Deputy Director of Development,
Royal Court Theatre, Sloane Square,
London, SW1W 8AS

Email: livnilssen@royalcourttheatre.com
Tel: 020 7565 5079

Young Vic
It's a big world in here

Our shows

We present the widest variety of classics, new plays, forgotten works and music theatre. We tour and co-produce extensively within the UK and internationally.

Our artists

Our shows are created by some of the world's great theatre people alongside the most adventurous of the younger generation. This fusion makes the Young Vic one of the most exciting theatres in the world.

Our audience

. . . is famously the youngest and most diverse in London. We encourage those who don't think theatre is 'for them' to make it part of their lives. We give 10 per cent of our tickets to schools and neighbours irrespective of box-office demand, and keep prices low.

Our partners near at hand

Each year we engage with 10,000 local people – individuals and groups of all kinds including schools and colleges – by exploring theatre on and off stage. From time to time we invite our neighbours to appear on our stage alongside professionals.

Our partners further away

By co-producing with leading theatre, opera and dance companies from London and around the world we create shows neither partner could achieve alone.

The Cut Bar and Restaurant

Our bar and restaurant is a relaxing place to meet and eat. An inspired mix of classic and original playthemed dishes made from fresh, free-range and organic ingredients creates an exciting menu.
www.thecutbar.com

The Young Vic is a company limited by guarantee, registered in England No. 1188209
VAT registration No. 236 673 348

The Young Vic (registered charity No 268876) received public funding from

markit™

Lead Sponsor of the Young Vic's Funded Ticket Scheme

Get More from the Young Vic online

Sign up to recieve email updates at youngvic.com/register

 youngvictheatre

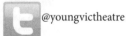 @youngvictheatre

 youngviclondon

 youngviclondon.wordpress.com

 @youngvictheatre

SUPPORTING THE YOUNG VIC

The Young Vic relies on the generous support of many individuals, trusts, foundations, and companies to produce our work, on and off stage. For their recent support we thank

PUBLIC FUNDERS

Arts Council England
British Council
Creative & Cultural Skills
Lambeth Borough Council
Southwark Council

CORPORATE PARTNERS

Barclays
Berkeley Group
Bloomberg
Edelman
Markit
Wahaca

CORPORATE MEMBERS

aka
Bloomberg
Clifford Chance
Edelman
Ingenious Media PLC
Memery Crystal
Mishcon de Reya
Royal Bank of Scotland
and NatWest
Wisdom Council

PARTNERS AND UPPER CIRCLE

Lionel Barber
The Bickertons
Tony & Gisela Bloom
Simon & Sally Borrows
Sandra Cavlov
Caroline & Ian Cormack
Manfred & Lydia Gorvy
Patrick Handley
Jack & Linda Keenan
Patrick McKenna
Simon & Midge Palley
Karl-Johan Persson
Barbara Reeves
Jon & NoraLee Sedmak
Dasha Shenkman
Justin Shinebourne
Rita & Paul Skinner
Bruno Wang
Anda & Bill Winters

SOUL MATES

David and Corinne Abbott
Jane Attias
Chris & Frances Bates
Ginny & Humphrey Battcock
Anthony & Karen Beare
Joanne Beckett
Royce & Rotha Bell
Sarah Billinghurst Solomon
Sarah Bunting
Lisa and Adrian Binks
Eva Boenders & Scott Stevens

Beatrice Bondy
Katie Bradford
CJ & LM Braithwaite
Simon Brych-Nourry
Clive and Helena Butler
Kay Ellen Consolver
Lucy & Spencer de Grey
Annabel Duncan-Smith
Sean Egan
Jennifer & Jeff Eldredge
Don Ellwood & Sandra Johnigan
Lysbeth Fox
Paul Gambaccini
Sarah Gay Fletcher
Jill and Jack Gerber
Beth & Gary Glynn
Rory Godson
Annika Goodwille
Sarah Hall
Katherine Hallgarten
Richard Hardman
& Family
Frances Hellman
Nick Hern
Madeleine Hodgkin
Nik Holttum & Helen Brannigan
Jane Horrocks
Linden Ife
Maxine Isaacs
Clive Jones
Tom Keatinge
John Kinder & Gerry Downey
Mr & Mrs Herbert Kretzmer
Carol Lake
Martha Lane Fox
Jude Law
Victoria Leggett
Chris & Jane Lucas
Tony Mackintosh
James & Sue Macmillan
Jill & Justin Manson
Lady Medina Marks
Michael McCabe
Karen McHugh
Sir Ian McKellen
Barbara Minto
Miles Morland
Georgia Oetker
Rob & Lesley O'Rahilly
Anthony & Sally Salz
Catherine Schreiber
Carol Sellars
Dr. Bhagat Sharma
Nicola Stanhope
Sir Patrick Stewart
Jan & Michael Topham
Totally Theatre Productions
The Ulrich Family
Donna & Richard Vinter
Jimmy & Carol Walker
Rob & Gillian Wallace
Edgar & Judith Wallner

TRUST SUPPORTERS

Amberstone Trust
Andor Charitable Trust
Austin & Hope Pilkington Trust
Backstage Trust
Boris Karloff Charitable Foundation
The City Bridge Trust
The Cleopatra Trust
Clifford Chance Foundation
Clore Duffield Foundation
Cockayne – Grants for the Arts
John S Cohen Foundation
The Dr. Mortimer and
Theresa Sackler Foundation
D'Oyly Carte Charitable Trust
Embassy of the Kingdom
of the Netherlands
Equitable Charitable Trust
The Eranda Foundation
Ernest Cook Trust
The Foyle Foundation
Garfield Weston Foundation
Garrick Charitable Trust
Genesis Foundation
Golden Bottle Trust
Golsoncott Foundation
The Harold Hyam Wingate Foundation
Jerwood Charitable Foundation
John Thaw Foundation
J. Paul Getty Jnr Charitable Trust
The Kidron and Hall Family
The Leche Trust
The Limbourne Trust
The London Community Foundation
The Mackintosh Foundation
The Martin Bowley Charitable Trust
The Noel Coward Foundation
The Portrack Charitable Trust
The Rayne Trust
The Red Hill Trust
Richard RadcliffeCharitable Trust
The Richenthal Foundation
Royal Victoria Hall Foundation
The Sackler Trust
Unity Theatre Trust
The Wolfson Foundation

and all other donors who wish to remain anonymous.

Cuttin' It

Charlene James trained at Birmingham School of Acting
and The School at Steppenwolf, Chicago. In 2008, she
participated in the Royal Court Young Writers Programme
and in 2012 she was selected to be one of the '503Five'
at Theatre503. In 2013 she became a writer in residence
at Birmingham Rep for their season focusing on mental
health. Her play *Tweet Tweet* was commissioned by the
Rep as part of Young Theatre Makers, and premiered
there before touring. Charlene was awarded the Alfred
Fagon Award for Best New Play at the National Theatre
for *Cuttin' It*, which also received the George Devine
Award in 2015.

CHARLENE JAMES

Cuttin' It

FABER & FABER

First published in 2016
by Faber and Faber Limited
74–77 Great Russell Street
London WC1B 3DA

Typeset by Country Setting, Kingsdown, Kent CT14 8ES
Printed in England by CPI Group (UK) Ltd, Croydon CR0 4YY

A CIP record for this book
is available from the British Library

ISBN 978-0-571-32963-2

2 4 6 8 10 9 7 5 3 1

Acknowledgements

Rosemarie James
for having stopped asking if
there'll be an interval in my plays

Caroline Tateo and Richard Blanco
for your brutal honesty from the very beginning

Lily Williams and Charlie Weedon
at Curtis Brown

The panel of the Alfred Fagon Award

The panel of the George Devine Award

David Lan and Ben Cooper at the Young Vic

The teams at the Young Vic, Birmingham Rep,
the Royal Court, Sheffield Crucible and The Yard

Gbolahan Obisesan

The team at Faber and Faber

Cuttin' It, a Young Vic and Royal Court Theatre co-production with Birmingham Repertory Theatre, Sheffield Theatres and The Yard Theatre, was first presented at the Young Vic on 20 May 2016 and at the Royal Court Jerwood Theatre Upstairs on 23 June 2016.

Muna Adelayo Adedayo
Iqra Tsion Habte

Direction Gbolahan Obisesan
Design Joanna Scotcher
Light Azusa Ono
Sound Adrienne Quartly
Casting Amy Ball
Voice Hazel Holder
Assistant Director Anastasia Osei-Kuffour
Design Assistant Daisy Young

Characters

Muna
fifteen years old, born in Somalia,
but raised in England since the age of three.
She has the accent of the English city she's from

Iqra
fifteen years old, born in Somalia,
moved to England at the age of ten.
She has a strong Somali accent

CUTTIN' IT

CHAPTER 11

The European Parliament
estimates 500,000 girls and women
living in Europe are suffering
with the lifelong consequences
of female genital mutilation.

Amnesty International, 2014

This story is for them.

Muna   Not again. I cannot be late again. I've taken
        liberties one too many times, an' this time they
        won't jus 'low it.

        It ain't even intentional. I set my alarm clock but
        it jus ain't alarmin enough, summat 'bout birds
        tweetin their iPhone song makes me wanna stay
        under the covers, tucked up warm in bed. But
        can't be doin with form-tutor stresses. Hearin
        that same tired line, tellin me to apply myself.

        Get a text from D'marnie askin me if I know that
        the bus don't run on brown-people time. So I
        hot foot it. Jessica Ennis it, still lookin pretty as
        I quick-step the pavement with the belief I'm
        gonna make it. I have to make it.

Iqra   8.17 a.m. The bus number 47. I sit downstairs,
        never upstairs. I like to look at the faces of the
        people out of the window. All different colours
        and shapes and sizes. But in their differences,
        they all have one thing the same. They are all
        miserable. As if they all agreed to get out of bed
        in the morning and be angry at the world. Maybe
        they hope that if they start their day badly, it will
        only get better.

Muna   Out of breath an' with a bit of a sweat on, I get
        there. I reach. My hand bangs on the door of
        the number 47 and Mr Bus Man takes one look
        at me – he looks at me like openin the doors of
        his bus to let people on ain't part of his job

description. Leavin me standin there, tryin to shame me. Denyin me my rights to get on the bus. I'm like that Rosa what's her name? But forget sittin down, I jus wanna get on.

Then this joker has the absolute audacity to pull off. He drives away without me.

Waste man.

Iqra I see her running. The whole bus sees her running. She has an audience. A top deck of grey-and-white uniform pressed against the windows, enjoying the show. She bangs on the door of the number 47, and I reach out and press the bell. But today, the driver has no mercy, and he pretends not to see her or hear me, and he drives on. Laughter roars out from the uniforms on the top deck. She shouts after him –

Muna Racist paedo!

It's true. My man's got too many shades of brown on his ride. Probably thinks the ones with the hoods are gonna stab him up an' the ones with the scarves are gonna blow him up. Idiot. If he can't handle it, he should jog on back to Poland, or wherever it is they're from. Ain't 'bout bein racist but I can't stand 'em, man, lookin at you like you're summat they found on the bottom of their shoe. I bet ya if I was some white girl standin here in this uniform, some blue-eyed, blonde-haired white girl, Mr Bus Man would be stoppin then, wouldn't he, stoppin to have a nice little look? I should report him. Watch me report him.

My phone beeps. Get a text from Makeda. It's in block capitals:

SHAME. LOL!

Iqra   I look behind me and she becomes smaller and smaller, as the bus number 47 continues on.

Muna   It's too early. I cannot be dealin with this when it's so early. I seriously consider jackin in the day, writin it off and startin again tomorrow – tomorrow's a new day an' all that. Today jus 'low me to jump back in bed an' forget it all, watch Jeremy Kyle an' eat some chocolate Hobnobs. But I don't want school admin conversin with my mum. Tryin to tell her I'm late again, skivin again, an' me havin to translate it all for her again. Givin my own English to Somali version:

'They're jus phonin to say how well I'm doin in school, Mum.'

Don't know if she'll fall for it again, an' it ain't worth the aggro, so I brave it. I walk it. New Primarks squeezin up my feet, but I soldier on.

Iqra   I do not know the answer. Whenever I do not know the answer, I daydream. If x equals 35, what is the value of y? Mr Dennis, my maths teacher with his round, pink face, tells me I must solve this problem. If x equals 35, what is the value of y? This is not a problem. It is a question to be answered, just numbers and letters on a page. I want to tell him about problems, real problems. I want to ask him when will x and y ever be useful for me? But of course, I do not. Instead my mind wanders. My imagination wakes and takes me back home.

I wipe dust from my eyes and look up to see my home demolished and a gun pressed against my mother's head. She is shaking but she tries to stay calm. She knows that if she cries, my brother will cry, and so will I, and we must never cry in front

17

of them. His leather skin is old and worn, even though he is half the age of my mother. I imagine his breath against her face is putrid. We learnt that word from a poem in English. Putrid. It means something foul-smelling – rotten. Saliva balls rest at the sides of his mouth, sticky and white, ready to spit out and attack. He leans closer in to her.

'I have demolished your home. I will make you watch as my men demolish your children, and then I will take my time and destroy you.'

She buckles to her knees. He grabs her neck and drags her back to standing position. Her scarf loosens and her thick, dark curls fall over her face. My brother jumps up and runs to her, but before he can reach her, a soldier takes a gun and butts him in the back of his head. I hear the crack as if it were my head. I see the blood as if it were my blood flowing from my own body.

He is still, and I scream.

'I know the answer.'

Twelve pairs of bloodshot eyes look at me. I have their attention. I yell out again. This time my voice cracks.

'y equals 6.'

No one moves.

'Are you sure?'

His eyes lock in to me, and I want to run, but the fear stops me.

I hear footsteps. They come closer and closer, until I can make out the figure of the person running from the horizon. It is Mr Dennis. His face is no longer pink, but red from the hot sun. He stands before me and pats me on the back, congratulating me.

'The girl is right. If x equals 35, then the value of y does equal 6.'

And just like that, the war is over. Mr Dennis looks at me; his shirt is soaked in sweat and his smile is wider than the ocean.

'See, Iqra.'

He says.

'Maths really counts.'

As I said . . . when will I ever need this?

Muna I get to the school gates an' check the time. It's practically the end of German. I think about goin in, arrivin all fashionably late an' that . . . but then I remember there ain't nuttin fashionable 'bout German, so I 'low it and wait it out by the 'bunk off' bus stop.

Play some Rihanna tunes on my phone, 'cause ain't no one else here – not even Amy Mitchell, an' Amy Mitchell's always here. She's this crazy white girl in our year who never comes to school. She's alright to hang out with though, 'cause she's got unlimited everythin on her phone – internet, minutes, texts, calls, the lot. Makeda said it's 'cause her dad had an affair, an' when her mum found out, she put her head in the oven an' killed herself. I guess her dad was all guilty an' that, so he got her a monthly unlimited plan. Can you imagine that? She is so lucky.

I can't wait to be grown and makin my own money, 'cause it ain't 'bout bein young and broke.

We're at that point in school where teachers keep harpin on 'bout what we gonna do with our lives, what direction we gonna take. I dunno. Every time I decide I wanna do summat, someone comes along an' puts me right off. Like the other day when I wanted to be a nurse, then Deanne McLean told me her mum's a nurse an' she has to put her finger up old men's bottoms. I ain't doin that. Even with gloves on, that's jus nasty.

I'm good at talkin an' that an' listenin to people. My friends always come to me to talk about their problems, and I'm the one who finds solutions to their stresses. I give 'em advice an' that. I guess I could be like, a counsellor or summat. But I'd really care about the people who come and see me, not like our school counsellor. She's this big, fat heifer everyone calls 'The Blimp'. More concerned with when she's gettin her next McDonald's fix than she is about our problems. Makeda said to me once that I was so good at listenin to people yeah, an' carin 'bout them, that if any of the girls in our year was bein touched up by their own dad or summat, they'd come an' talk to me about it, rather than go to The Blimp . . . which is probably true, 'cause if you can't tell yourself to put the Big Mac down, how can you be tryin to dish out advice to anyone else?

She gets herself ready to go into school.

The only thing about listenin an' dealin with everyone else's problems, though, is that no one's there to listen to yours. An' right 'bout now, I wish I did have someone to talk to.

Iqra   I sit alone in the school canteen, wishing very much that it was my mother's food I was eating.

It has been four months and six days since I came to John Lansbury Secondary. I am still the new girl. It is an effort for people to talk to me and to get to know me. They already have their friends. There is no room in their groups for the 'freshie' with the accent.

Muna They're servin jerk chicken and 'reggae hot beans' today.

Makeda said her grandma would jump out her grave and slap the school cook for callin that dryness jerk chicken – but that don't stop her eatin it though. Can't stomach it. Ain't hungry. Push my plate away an' D'marnie attacks the chips like a vulture. Between mouthfuls she's talkin 'bout how her sister got stopped outside Topshop. Some guy gave her a card askin if she wants to be a model an' he told D'marnie, yeah, that she could pass for Rihanna – without the acne, obviously. I love these girls, bffs an' all that. But sometimes even with mates, you can't tell them everythin that's goin on with you.

Iqra I am the girl who has no parents any more, no brothers left. The girl living with a woman she calls her aunt, but isn't her aunt. I am the girl who has been through a real-life war, like the war they see on their televisions – the films, the news. I want to forget all that but they will not let me. They give me a school counsellor to talk to. They think it will help me if I talk to the whale lady whose office is at the back of the PE cupboard. That woman has no idea what I went through. She sits sipping from a Diet Coke can pretending to make the effort, when I see the crumbs of the cookies she ate moments before I arrived to our special session together.

I learnt that it is not for me that they do it, it is for them. They do not want me breaking down in the halls screaming for my dead family when this Ofsted come. But I do not want to be called out of history class to talk about war with anyone. I want to be left alone. I wish the girls in my year would pass on to the teachers what they have already discovered.

I am not worth the attention.

Muna   Final bell of the day is like music to my ears, it sings out that I'm free. Home time. Laters.

I get to the bus stop an' it's the usual bus stop shenanigans. Boys carryin on stupid tryin to impress the girls. Girls standin unimpressed. I stand back so I don't fall victim to one of their juvenile pranks. Today ain't the day to be testin me, you get me.

I see Keda and Marnie but I ain't in the mood to chat breeze or to listen to their gas. I got too much to deal with. So I message 'em, say I got after-school detention.

Bus comes and a sea of grey and white uniform swarm like they got cooked food waitin for them at home. I wait for the mob to storm the stairs and take their seats on the top deck. Mr Bus Man ain't the same bus man who started my day wrong, and for that, this bus man is lucky. I sit downstairs. I never sit downstairs. Feels weird. I find a seat, one of them awkward facin-backwards seats that gets you touchin toes an' brushin knees with some stranger you'd rather not be doin that with. I put my headphones in an' try an' escape these thoughts that won't leave my head. Flick the tracks but the music ain't helpin. I can't stop thinkin 'bout how small an' innocent she is. I consider for a sec goin upstairs with D'marnie and Makeda, listen to them chat lots 'bout nothin. Let 'em clear my mind.

She catches my eye. Sat in the back with me like she's escapin summat too – jus wants to be left. She's in one of my classes, can't remember which. Never spoke to her. Heard all the rumours 'bout her though. She makes me feel like I got away with summat. I mean, we're both the same age an' both born in the same country an' that, but I'm the one who got away. I've never known what she's known, an' she's only gettin to know what I know now, an' that ain't fair. We're opposites, even though we came from the same, she's nothin like me, an' that shames me.

She's got this fake 'Hello Kitty' bag which she's way too old for. It's summat my little sister would like. Summat she'd see in the Argos catalogue and say,

'Muna, this is what I want for my birthday. Do you remember that it's my birthday comin up? It's nearly here, Muna, it's nearly here.'

Like I can forget.

My stomach gets tighter.

Iqra   Her head presses against the window of the bus as the beat escapes her earphones. I sit like a statue, hoping she will not notice me, but deep down I hope that she will. I decide to myself that if she looks, I will smile at her. She flicks from one song to another then another. I suddenly catch her eye and my heart is in my mouth. I forget to smile and she looks away. Her eyes fall

to my bag, this stupid kiddie bag, then they dart
back to me and they look away again. Out of the
window I see her reflection and I wonder to
myself if we would have been the best of friends
if we were back home. But here, we are sitting
like strangers. Worlds apart.

Muna I look out the window, but don't really look,
don't take it in. I'm thinkin 'bout her.

My little sister's birthday comin.

She's so excited. Says she's bored of bein six now,
she's ready to be seven. She got Mum to buy the
huge tin of chocolate Celebrations to hand out to
her school friends already. I remember bein seven.
Won't be the same for her.

Iqra I look in front of me, I keep my eyes forward so
they do not look at hers. But out of the corner
of my eye, I see her with her head placed back,
taking in slow, deep breaths like she is trying to
suck up all the air on the bus. This is my stop.

Muna I think I'm gonna vom. Travellin backwards
ain't agreein with me, thoughts in my head ain't
agreein with me. I get up. We both reach for the
bell at the same time. This ain't my stop, but I
need to get off 'cause I'm gettin dizzy – should've
eaten summat at lunch. Feel her hand on my
shoulder, as she helps me off the bus. I take a
deep breath, fresh air hits my lungs. Feels good.
Feels like I could still spew, but I don't, 'cause
that would be embarrassin, so I jus keep breathin
slow an' deep. She puts her hand in her pocket
an' offers me a sweet. Like the kind you get back
in Somalia, the kind my grandma used to give
me. I take it.

Iqra	'Are you okay?'

Muna 'Yeah. Thanks.'

Iqra 'You don't look very good. Maybe you should sit down.'

Muna 'Okay.'

Iqra 'You should eat the mint.'

Muna 'Thanks.'

Iqra 'It will make you feel better.'

Muna Feel ashamed that I didn't take the time to speak to her before, an' now she's here helpin me when she don't have to. Her voice is gentle like my grandma. Makes me wanna hug her – but I don't 'cause she might think I'm weird. After thank you, I don't really know what to say. Start to read the graffiti on the bus stop.

Iqra My father used to bring these sweets for me and my brothers. Green and blue wrappers that made a crackling sound when you rub them in your hand.

If I was upset, he would call me to him and give me a sweet and pat me on the head. Then everything would be okay.

Now I am the one dishing out sweets.

I pick at my fingers and wonder how blood always gets behind my fingernails.

Awkward silence.

Muna 'What's your name?'

Iqra 'Iqra.'

Muna 'I'm Muna.'

Iqra   'I know.'

We have the same English class together. I sit behind her in the same English class every week. I know who she is and I definitely know her name.

Muna   'Your sweets remind me of Somalia.'

Iqra   'Where are you from?'

Muna   'Lakeview Gardens. Ain't that far from here.'

Iqra   'Where in Somalia are you from?'

Muna   'Oh, right . . . yeah. Erm. Kismaayo.'

Iqra   'Me too.'

Muna   'Really?'

Iqra   'I lived there before I went to the camp.'

Muna   'The camp?'

Iqra   'The refugee camp.'

Muna   'Oh.'

Then there's this proper awkward silence. 'Cause what do you say to that?

'Sorry.'

Iqra   'It is okay.'

Muna   'If you ever wanna, you know, hang out or anythin – not that hangin out with me's gonna make up for you bein in a refugee camp or anythin – I jus meant, you know, if you ever want to talk or anythin –'

Iqra   'Thank you.'

Muna   I ain't gonna open my mouth again, not to let some foolishness escape like I got verbal diarrhoea.

So I take out my iPod, sit a bit closer to her, give her the left earphone an' keep the right. Press play.

She listens to the song like it's the first time she's heard it.

Iqra I like the part where she sings 'You are beautiful . . . like a diamond in the sky.'

Muna Song ends.

'You can borrow it if you want. Some proper good tunes on there.'

She grins like a little kid as I hand it over.

Iqra 'I will take very good care of it. Thank you, Muna. Thank you.'

Muna She thanks me like a thousand times. It's old anyway.

'I better get goin.'

Iqra 'Are you feeling better?'

Muna 'Yeah, cheers. Much better, thanks.'

Iqra 'Good. Okay –'

Muna 'I've gotta go home. Stuff to do an' that.'

Iqra 'Yes, I understand.'

Muna 'Thanks for the sweet, yeah.'

I stand up too fast, nearly trip over her fake Kitty bag. We both reach to pick it up. I get there first. Hold it in my hands an' it reminds me of her an' it all comes floodin back.

Iqra 'Are you okay?'

Muna 'No.'

Iqra	'What is wrong?'
Muna	Don't know if I should tell her. Don't know how to. I feel my chest gettin all tight like I can't breathe, like it's gonna explode if I don't just get it out. Tryin to make sense of it, tryin to find the words, but the tears are buildin up, they're wellin up.

So I just say it.

'My little sister's birthday soon. She's gonna be seven.'

'I think . . . I think they're gonna cut her.'

First time I said that out loud. Hurt to say it, pained me to say it.

'I jus thought that you . . . you know . . . that I can tell you 'cause you understand. I – I –'

I can't finish. I have to walk away before I cry, 'cause if I start to cry, I know I ain't gonna stop an' it ain't 'bout me bawlin on the road for everyone to see.

Iqra	'Muna!'
Muna	I hear her call me, but I don't acknowledge it. Don't look back. Don't stop. Don't even know why I told her. Don't know why I'm chattin my business to someone I jus met. Thought I might feel better talkin 'bout it, gettin it off my chest an' that, but I don't. I feel like there's this burnin in me, an' it's gettin hotter an' I'm gettin fired up. I wanna get home, an' have it out with her. Jus need to get home.

My steps turn into strides, an' as I hot foot the pavement, I jus wanna scream, let it all out. Like proper scream an' make them all hear me.

I wanna scream out past these estate walls. I want my voice to reach. I wanna be heard in the villages. I want every woman, every mother – I want my mother to hear my screams and know that it's time to stop, 'cause what they're doin ain't okay, I need to scream it out, what they're doin ain't right.

Iqra I want to run after her, bring her back here and ask her what is wrong – what is upsetting her. But she is gone.

I walk towards the estate in front of me, the block of flats where I live faces me. It is an ugly building. It is a sad, grey, concrete building. They say that the man who designed it jumped off it after it was finished. I do not know if this is true or not. The lift, with its constant stench of urine and dog faeces, never works. It is always 'out of order' and 'sorry for the inconvenience'.

The door to the entrance of my block has been forced open and there is broken glass over the floor. It has been there since yesterday. Someone made an attempt to clean it up, but scattered pieces still remain. There are children living here. It would not take much for them to get hurt, to get cut.

People here should be more careful.

Muna I get home. I reach. I'm out of breath an' with a sweat on. Tears have dried and stained my face, leavin white marks round my eyes, like I ain't creamed my face this mornin, like Vaseline don't live in this house.

I hear my little sister upstairs. I usually go up, greet them. Hear 'bout her day. Hear 'bout how

29

the Romans invaded Britain, or how her friend
Sowda got in trouble for talkin in class again. But
not today. Today I'm on a mission. Fire burnin
in my belly. I go straight to the kitchen an' start
openin cupboards an' drawers – doubt they'll be
in between the cereal boxes, but I search there
anyway. My mum hears the commotion an'
comes downstairs. Good. I turn and face her.

'Mahaa da-ay?' (*What's going on?*)

She wants to know what's goin on, so I tell her
in English. She don't like us speakin English at
home, wants us to keep up the Somali, afraid
we're losin our identity. I ask her where she's put
them, takes her a while to understand, to keep up
with me.

'Mahaa tidi?' (*What are you saying?*)

She speaks in Somali. Wants to know what I'm
saying. I speak in English.

'Where are the tickets?'

Tells me she don't understand. Dunno if she
means the English, or she don't understand what
I'm talkin 'bout.

The fire builds, it burns.

'The plane tickets you bought to take her away.'

Keeps shakin her head not understandin an' her
confusion leads to my frustration.

'I know you're takin her away, 'cause that's what
you do – it's what you did to me. Turn seven an'
you take us away.'

Now she understands.

'No Somalia.'

She says this in English.

'We don't go Somalia. I don't take her.'

I catch my breath. Try to swallow, but can't.

'You're not sendin her?'

'No Somalia.'

Tells me we ain't goin. I make her promise me.
She looks me in my eyes an' says we ain't goin.
Tells me we can't afford it. I ain't never been so
happy in my whole life to be broke. Make her
promise me again and again.

'She's stayin here then, yeah? You're not takin
her?'

Keep askin and she keeps sayin no. Gotta be sure
an' when I feel sure, I sit down. Put my hands to
my head and breathe deep.

Hear her footsteps bombin it down the stairs.
She calls out to me. Plaster my face in a smile so
she don't see me stressed. Look up and see her
standin there, hands holdin summat behind her
back. School uniform lookin like it was in a food
fight an' lost.

'Got somethin to show you.'

Her hands come forward to reveal this big book
she's holdin, covered in some wallpaper. Written
in her best glitter pen, it says, 'My Birthday
Presents'. It's the Argos catalogue. She's decorated
the Argos catalogue, 'cause she's nearly seven an'
she's got too much time on her hands. She flicks
through the pages, and stops at the kids' section,
the toy section. Pushes it towards me.

'I've circled what I want for my birthday.'

I look down at the page, then back at her. She smiles. I turn the next page, an' the next. She's circled everythin. The whole lot of it's on her wish list. Yeah, you wish.

I look at her. Remember when she was born, Dad took me to the hospital. The whole way there he wouldn't tell me if I had a sister or a little brother 'cause he wanted it to be a surprise. I remember sittin in the car with every part of me crossed, prayin for a boy, pleadin it was a boy – please Allah, give me a little brother. Got there an' saw my mum holdin this baby wrapped up in this pink blanket, an' I lost it, I jus started to cry. They thought I was jealous, couldn't handle not bein the only child any more. But they were wrong, 'cause I knew what it meant to have a little sister. I knew what it meant for her.

Now she's standin here, my little sister, with this massive grin on her face, like three of her teeth ain't missin out her mouth.

Know I prayed for a brother, but wouldn't change a thing about her now. I love her to bits. I hug her into me. Hold on an' squeeze her a bit too tight. Can't let her go. Don't want to let her go. She's my little sister. An' it's gonna be different for her.

Iqra I live on floor number nine, so that is 144 steps to climb. For me, I do not mind, I like to walk the stairs. I do not like the lift. There is something about the door closing and trapping me inside that scares me. I prefer the stairs. But I think suddenly to myself that 144 steps is a long way to climb for little legs and feet, and I wonder if their mothers ever carry them.

A hundred and forty, hal-afar-hal (*141*), 142, hal-afar-sadeh (*143*), 144. I go between Somali and English as I walk up each step. I do not know why I do this.

Number 97. I open the door. The smell no longer overwhelms me. It is a smell now that I am used to, I am familiar with. It has now become the perfume, soaking and staining every wall, filling every room. I enter the flat and I am standing in the sitting room. When I first arrived here, I asked if it was called the sitting room because of all the chairs in here. Twelve seats line the walls of the room. Stools, upturned crates, broken chairs.

There are two bedrooms in the flat, a large one and a small one. I sleep in the small one. There is no decoration on the walls, no colour, no life. Two pieces of material hang from the window and act as a curtain. They do not come together and meet where they are supposed to, so the early morning light creeps through, not letting me sleep past 5 a.m.

This is the room we share together. Hers and mine. On the floor, two mattresses lie next to each other. Both exactly the same, worn and old, covered by a single sheet and a pillow.

Under her pillow she keeps a small envelope. Each night before she goes to sleep, with her back turned to me, she takes out the envelope, inside it are three photographs. Once, when she was not here, I opened the envelope and looked at the faces. Faces of people she cares about, photos of people she loves. Maybe a husband, her children, friends, her family. At night I lie back on my mattress, squeeze close my eyes and try to see the faces of my family, of the people I love. Three of my brothers I no longer remember. I can no longer see them in my head. They have gone. I am their surviving sister and I am meant to carry their memory on, but I cannot remember their faces. Before I fall asleep, I say each of their names over and over because I have forgotten their faces, but I will not forget their names.

Sometimes when she sleeps she holds the photos close to her heart, and cries a tiny cry that she thinks I cannot hear. But I do hear it and it is deafening. It reminds me of what I have lost. So, when she cries, I take my bed sheet and I creep into the sitting room to leave her with her grief.

There is another mattress in the large room, but that is not where I go. I never sleep in there.

I use the upturned crate as a rest for my head and I throw the sheet over me and curl up on the floor of the sitting room, like the girls who come and wait.

She calls out my name to see if it is me back home from school. An auntie who is not my auntie. I am only here because neither of us now has anyone else. I am here to help her work.

I call to her that the bus was late.

She comes to the door. Once she had a beautiful face and a beautiful smile, but all that is gone now.

She tells me to finish my school work. Numbers and letters on a page.

I smile to myself. I have been four months and seven days at John Lansbury, and now I have Muna, my new friend.

I take out her music player and press play.

'Beautiful like diamonds in the sky.'

Muna   Get up early this mornin – get up before my
alarm clock – well, not before it, but only had to
press the snooze button once.

I get on the early bus thinkin she'd be on it.
Excited for her to be on it. She ain't. Sit downstairs
an' wait for her to get on, but she don't show.
Walk through the school gates an' teachers nearly
have a heart attack seein me reach before 5 to 9.
Form tutor nearly spits out her porridge seein me
arrive before time.

'Are you okay?' 'Has something happened?'

'Turnin over a new leaf, miss.'

Leave her standin there in disbelief with her coffee-
breath mouth wide open, like she's catchin flies.

Iqra   She tells me that I will not be going to school
today. She has to go out and there is work to be
done here. There is cleaning to be done here.
I change back out of my uniform. I never work
in my school uniform.

It is very difficult to explain how the mix of
bleach and blood have stained your clothes.

Muna   Need to see her an' make sure she don't think I'm
crazy for cryin on the street like that. I need to
see her an' make sure she ain't told nobody.

Wanna tell her my sister's safe. She's gonna be okay.

Iqra   She likes everything to be clean. It is important
that everything is clean. She has her particular

way of how this should be done. It takes time and it takes care.

Muna Thinkin of invitin her to my sister's party. A way of sayin thanks for bein there an' listenin an' that. Dunno, could be alright hangin out with her. But I don't see her, I can't find her to ask her. So I speak to Annis, this boy from the year below, lives round her way, gets off at the same stop as her. He gives me the name of her block an' her number an' I go round there after school.

Iqra All day I prepare the rooms and I listen to songs on Muna's music player. Her gift to me. I want to see her and shower her with blue and green wrappers, with all the sweets in Somalia. Anything to make her feel better, anything to make sure she is okay.

Muna Get to her estate after school and find her block. It's proper depressin, proper ugly here. Cement should be used for pavements and car parks, not for decoratin outside of people's homes. Thought I lived in a right dive, but there's always someone worse off than you, ain't there?

Go to press the buzzer at the entrance, but don't need to, door's already open. Door's been busted open. Tread on some glass as I walk in. Good job I ain't wearin my Primarks today, 'cause if glass would've cut up my foot, I would be cussin.

Lift smells rank, ain't 'bout goin in there. Then I realise how many floors there are, how many steps there are. Definitely ain't 'bout doin that. Step inside the lift, hold my nose 'cause it smells like some cats had a right piss party in here. Press number nine. See the notice too late. 'Out of order. Sorry for the inconvenience.' Summat sticky on

36

my finger. I wipe it along the walls as I climb the never-endin steps.

I reach the top an' I have to catch my breath before I knock the door.

Iqra There is a knock on the door. It scares me. She is not in, but she always uses her key when she returns. I am here by myself. I am alone. Never answer the door to anyone. The same rule in Somalia applies here too. So just like in Somalia, I sit on the floor and hold my breath until they have gone.

Muna I knock like forever, but she ain't answerin and I don't really wanna face treadin all them steps again. So I try again, call her name. Maybe she's in her bedroom at the back listenin to music, headphones in an' can't hear the door. Mum always has a go at me for that too.

Iqra I hear her call me. She calls my name.

Muna 'Iqra.'

Iqra 'Muna.'

I jump up and open the door to her without thinking, without realising what I have done.

Muna She opens the door and suddenly I don't know what to say. What is it 'bout this girl that gets me all awkward?

Iqra She stands looking at me. I should not have opened the door. I was not thinking. What if she wants to come in? She cannot come in.

Muna See, when I feel nervous an' awkward an' stuff, sense don't pass these lips. So I don't carry on normal and say, 'Hello' or 'You alright Iqra?

How's your day been?' Nah, none of that. What comes out my babblin mess of a mouth is,

'All them steps make me wanna do a wee. I'm proper burstin. Can I use your loo please?'

She don't say nuttin for a sec, shoulda jus left it there, but I ask again.

'I ain't gonna do a number two, I promise, it's jus a wee – I'd never come into someone's yard and violate it like that. I swear it's jus a wee.'

Sometimes I wish I knew when to stop chattin.

Iqra   I have to let her in. She will not stop talking about what will happen if she does not get to a toilet.

Muna   Soon as I step in, there's this – I can smell this smell comin from one of the rooms. It's overwhelmin. Hits me at the back of my throat, makes me wanna gag, makes me wanna get some Febreze an' douse the place. But I don't let on. Don't wanna seem rude when she's invited me in. Summat 'bout that smell though, recognise that smell, jus don't know how.

Try an' make conversation to keep my mind off it, but it's hard. Ask her how come she's got so many chairs in her livin room. Tells me her aunt does work with the Somali women in the community. She sounds nice.

Iqra   I walk her to the toilet and wait outside. I pray that she will hurry up and leave. My heart beats a bit faster every minute she is in there. I should not have let her in.

Muna   Come out the toilet. She's standin right there waitin for me. Makes me jump.

'You alright?'

Iqra   'You need to go.'

Muna   'Yeah, sorry 'bout jus turnin up on your doorstep. Jus wanted to talk 'bout what happened an' that.'

Iqra   'You cannot be here. I will get into trouble if you are here. I am not allowed people to come.'

Muna   'Yeah, my mum can be like that too. Never likes Keda an Marnie comin round.'

Iqra   'I need for you to go.'

Muna   She hurries me to the door and I can smell that smell again. It's like proper comin alive an' foll;win us. For a sec, I can't breathe. Don't want to breathe. Don't want that stink inhaled in me. That stink . . . don't know how I know it, but I definitely know it. Gets to my head.

    I jus need a minute.

Iqra   She stops in the living room. This is a mistake.

Muna   'I jus wanted to . . . you know . . . talk to someone who knows. Someone who understands. Not like I can chat to D'marnie or Makeda 'bout any of this stuff.'

Iqra   'I need for you to go.'

Muna   This ain't comin out right. Don't sound like it sounded when it was in my head.

    'Look, sorry for comin round, yeah. Sorry for botherin ya.'

    I go to leave.

Iqra   I cannot let her leave. She is my friend.

    'How is your sister?'

Muna I stop.

'It's all good. She's good. It's all gonna be fine, Iqra, that's what I came to tell ya.'

She doesn't look at me. Looks away. Stares down at the floor.

Then she says it.

Iqra 'You know, it is better for her that she gets cut now rather than later.'

Muna My stomach drops.

'What?'

Iqra 'Later will be painful for her.'

Muna Not sure I'm hearin her right. Ask her to repeat it.

Iqra 'Later will be painful for her, but now –'

Muna Is she serious? Is this girl standin in front of me chattin serious? 'It will be painful for her later, but now –'

'Now what?' I ask her.

'But now what, Iqra? She's six years old, you think she's not gonna feel anything?'

Iqra 'It is much better when they are young.'

Muna 'Better? Can you actually hear yourself? Better for who? For the elders who are gonna pin her down? Is it them you think it's best for 'cause she ain't got that much fight in her? Let me ask you this Iqra: was it better that they got me young too? Women that I'm supposed to look up to an' trust, throwin me down, pinnin me on the hard floor with their vice-grip hands. Clampin my shoulders back, diggin their heavy knees pressin an' bruisin up my chest. Was that supposed to be better for me? Pullin up my dress an' cuttin me. Havin her mutilate me?'

'I'll tell you now, none of that was best for me. An' none of that's gonna be best for my sister. Do you understand?'

Iqra 'It has to be done.'

Muna 'Why?'

Iqra 'Why?'

Muna 'Yeah, why does it have to be done?'

Iqra 'Because you are Muslim –'

Muna 'Ain't got nuttin to do with being Muslim –'

Iqra 'It is important for you to be clean –'

Muna 'Says nuttin in any part of the Quran 'bout cuttin up girls so they can stay clean. It's jus summat your mum told you 'cause that's what her mum told her, an' hers before that. Jus some messed-up tradition that needs to be broken.'

Iqra 'No –'

Muna 'Yes –'

Iqra 'If she does not have it done, she will not become a decent woman.'

Muna 'Do you know my sister? Have you met my sister? That little girl is more than decent . . . She's perfect just the way she is. So don't chat to me 'bout growin up to be a decent woman. A decent woman in whose eyes?'

Iqra 'In the eyes of our community.'

Muna 'So you think it's alright what they did to you? You think it's okay what they did to me and what they're still doin to all them little girls? Is it really okay that our community does that?'

Looks me right in the face.

Iqra 'It is not about being wrong or right. Who are we to question it? It is just what has to happen.'

Muna '*Who are we to question it*?'

Iqra For the first time, I hear out loud how that sounds.

Muna 'Who are we not to question it?'

Iqra I put my hand in my pocket and hear the crackle of the sweet wrappers.

Muna Don't know if it's 'cause I can smell that smell again, or if it's her with her back-home mentality that I wish she would have left back home. Thinkin it's okay, believin it's okay to mess summat up that don't have no business bein messed up, summat that should jus be left well alone. Don't know if it's the suffocatin stink or the frustration of her ignorance that makes my legs buckle and unsteady me. She makes a face, looks at me weird. Asks if I'm okay. Ask her if she can open a window, let some air in. See her move to the window fast. Hear the sounds of outside fill the room. Feel the coolness of the fresh air hit my skin.

Jus before I fall.

Iqra She passes out on my living-room floor. This is something that is not new to me. I place one of the cushions behind her head and fetch a damp rag from the kitchen to cool her down. I do not know how I will explain this if she walks in and sees her here like this.

I sit next to her patting the wet cloth on her head and I wait for her to wake.

She lies there so peacefully. I whisper in her ear, and hope she can hear me.

'I was six years old. I was young too.'

I had been playing with my brother Hdafur in the yard. Run and catch. I was always too slow for my brothers and they soon get bored of playing with me. I watched Hdafur run to the back of the house and slowly creep away again with a banana in his hand. Within seconds he was gone. I followed Hdafur's path to the bench at the back of the house. Occasionally, a neighbour would leave fruit on the bench, sometimes a bag of oranges, sometimes bananas. I looked around, there was nobody there, so I ripped one of the bananas from the bunch. I peeled back the yellow skin and took a bite. As soon as I did, my mother's voice roared into my ear. Like the banana, I almost jumped out of my skin.

'Those bananas are for your father. You are stealing from your own father.'

She looked down at me with such disappointment. I will never forget that look she gave to me.

The next day, my mother and I got on a bus to Mogadishu. I loved going on bus journeys. There was always so much to see.

No matter how much I begged and pleaded with my mother, she would not tell me why we were going. She just said it was for a special reason.

We arrived at a house I had never been to before. I did not know this house or who lived in it.

'We have come to see your aunties.'

That was all my mother told me.

'But all my aunties are back home.'

She hushed me and we entered.

I remember holding on to my mother's hand when I heard a young girl screaming at the back of the house. I turned to her frightened. She held me firmly by my shoulders and she looked into my eyes and said,

'Iqra, I hope you will not scream and carry on like that silly girl. You must be brave, Iqra. No crying. Do you understand?'

I nodded even though I did not understand. Why did I need to be brave to see my new aunties? What was going to happen to me? All I could think of was that girl and her screams. What were they doing to her to make her scream like that? I did not want to find out.

A lady came to collect us. She nodded her head and led us to the back room. It was a hot day. I remember feeling thirsty, but not daring to ask for a glass of water.

There were four elders in the room, and each of them grabbed a part of me and held me down on the floor. I was too scared to shout and too confused to scream, so I just lay there. A fifth elder came into the room and knelt down before me. She pulled my knickers down and forced my knees wide apart. I began to cry and my legs started to tremble. Every time I tried to close them, they would hold them back open with more force. The elder in front of me took out a small razor blade from her pocket. I yelled out to my mother and she whispered into my ear that

44

I must be brave. I must be very brave. The tears rolled down my cheeks, and I notice they rolled down hers too. I whispered back at my mother that I was sorry for taking the banana.

Then I felt the pain. An excruciating pain that took over my whole body. I kicked out at the one holding the razor blade and watched as blood shot from out of my body into her face and eyes. She did not flinch. She stopped slicing me for a moment and used her apron to wipe the blood away. My blood. As if it were drops of rain that had fallen from the sky on to her face. I wondered how many other girls had their blood stained on that apron.

The feeling afterwards was like my body was not mine any more. It felt alien to me. I did not want anything to do with it. Then I was stitched up, tied up and left to heal. My mother knelt beside me and said today I have become a woman. She smiled at me and through all the pain I tried to smile too.

I wait for Muna to wake.

We do it because it is our culture. We have done it for so long. It is who we are. It has to happen.

How can that be wrong?

I try and be different from them. I smile at the girls. Calm them, make it okay. Because no one made it okay for me.

Muna Today is summat new. Today is weekend. Little sister's birthday today an' she's excited, like it's excitin to be seven.

Yeah, I get it.

She's been up an' excited since five o'clock this mornin, singin a croaky 'Happy Birthday' to herself, stinkin out the room with her mornin breath. I let her open my present first. A sparkly tiara. Her eyes light up brighter than the plastic, pink jewels stuck on it. Asks me to put it on her.

Got home and realised I still had her damp, beige rag all bunched up in my hand. Didn't wanna think about where the stains on it came from, or what she used it for. My mum would have told me to wash it with the good soap and give it back to her the next day. Show my gratitude. I didn't want to see her the next day, or the day after that, so I put her dirty, used-out rag in the bin.

We're in the kitchen. Little sister's dressed as the latest Disney princess. Mum's gettin her ready to go to some party. She's dancin round the table tellin me about some kid from after-school club who's got the same birthday as her. So while Mum drops her off I'm gonna be here makin fairy cakes an' chocolate bakes ready for when she gets back to open her presents. Made a banner last week in geography instead of doin geography, gonna put that up. Wanna make it special for her.

A day to remember.

Iqra   They'll never forget this day. This day that seems so ordinary. Drops of rain are being spat from the sky. I wonder how many of them will remember that. I get the washed towels ready. They smell of cotton linen and are soft against my skin. I hope the rain does not fall too heavy today, because after they all leave, I will go to the high street to get the shopping.

Muna Soon as they leave, I put my music on, turn it up full blast. Been perfectin my party playlist – even got some Somali tunes on there. See if I can get my mum's sash swayin to the beat a little. I got all these important decisions to make. Popcorn or Pringles? Sisin or halwad? OJ or tropical mix? She's left her tiara on the table. I bet she's screwin. Bet she's tellin my mum to turn back and get it 'cause a princess can't turn up to a party without her tiara all sparklin and pretty.

Iqra When we first got here, there were not as many girls. Now more come. It used to be just one or two girls, now we have parties of five or six. It is cheaper for them that way. They come in groups and they save themselves money. They used to send for the elders in Somalia to come, fly them all the way over here. But now they have us. We provide the service for a fraction of the price.

I like this moment right now. The moment before they begin to arrive. It is so peaceful, so calm. All I hear is the murmur of a prayer from her.

She prays that nothing will go wrong.

Muna Get a text from Makeda wishin my little sis a happy birthday with seven kisses. Don't hear from D'marnie, but she ain't ever got any credit.

It's hard not bein able to tell your best mates everythin about you, but jus 'cause they're your mates, don't mean they're gonna understand. Not even I understand. What if they find out an' don't wanna roll with me no more? They think I'm a freak or summat? I'd miss them too much to tell them.

Iqra There is not a particular order. No list up with their names. It is just whoever pays first gets seen first. They sit in the living room, and after I have offered them some sweet tea I take their money and their daughter is next. Some of the mothers stay with them and some of the mothers go. I hold their child's hand and lead them off to the large room as I tell their mothers to come back in an hour.

It will all be over in an hour.

Muna Finish puttin out the paper plates an' Mum tells me the taxi's waitin outside.

'What taxi?'

She tells me the taxi to pick my sister up.

'Why we goin in a taxi?'

She tells me to hurry 'cause it's waitin for us. It's only been forty-five minutes. What kinda party finishes after forty-five minutes – even if they are only seven? Feel sorry for that kid, 'cause her party sounds dry. Lucky for my sister, the party I'm givin her is gonna be off the chain. Maybe I'll put out the popcorn as well as the Pringles. Go for it. You're only seven once.

Mum ain't said a word the whole journey. Jus keeps lookin down at her hands. Not answerin my questions.

'Where we goin?'

'How come we're in a taxi – we never get a taxi anywhere?'

'How come I have to be here?'

Jus keeps lookin down at her hands.

Iqra   The screams have already begun. If they have to scream, which they always do, they scream into a scrunched-up cloth that I bring to them. I hope that way, the ones who are waiting will not hear, but this is never guaranteed.

There are six of them here today. All young and nervous. Waiting, but not knowing what they are waiting for. I offer them a sweet, pat their heads and smile. A handful of blue-and-green wrappers. It should be easier for me today. The younger ones are over with much quicker.

Muna   Taxi man pulls over. Stops. I know this place. Why have we stopped here? This is Iqra's place. Can see her cement tower block tall in front of me.

'Why are we here?'

She's still lookin down at her hands.

An' then I feel it. That sick feelin in my stomach. That gut-wrenchin feelin in the pit of my belly.

I know why I'm here.

Ask her what number the party's at. Shout at her.

'What number's the party at?'

She tells me the same number as Iqra's door an' I suddenly taste the vomit in my mouth. Could be jus a coincidence. Maybe it ain't what I'm thinkin. Don't have to be what I'm thinkin jus 'cause I'm thinkin it.

'What have you done to her?'

She don't answer me. I scream at her.

'Tell me what you've done.'

She slowly lifts her head an' looks up at Iqra's tower block. Don't even wait for her to say the

49

words, 'cause I remember how I know that smell an' I race out the car an' over to her buildin with the hope I ain't too late.

Remember it proper vivid now. Antiseptic an' stale blood mixed with the heat of that day. Remember layin there cryin, smellin that smell, breathin it, inhalin it in after they doused me with the stuff, burnin me with the stuff. An' I'm feelin the tears burnin my eyes now, as I'm pleadin an' prayin it ain't too late.

Iqra   Most of them do not know what will happen when they are here. I hear their mothers tell them that this is an important day for them, a day they will become women. They do not know what this means.

Some of them are excited. They have been told that this is a special day where they will receive gifts and special treats. All they have to do is be brave. They must be brave little girls. The look between mother and daughter afterwards is always one of betrayal and guilt. No treat in the world was worth the pain.

Muna   Storm the stairs an' only feel my legs crampin once I reach the top. Ain't got no time for weakness in my body. I gotta be strong. For her. I catch my breath.

I'm stood in front of her door. Jus stand there lookin at her door. Don't wanna think 'bout what's happenin on the other side. Don't want it to be the truth. Take a deep breath, hope I'm wrong. Hopin I embarrass myself for gettin it so wrong. Hopin she gets all offended an' asks me to leave her house 'cause what I'm thinkin is so completely wrong.

Pound the door with my fists, like what they do in the films. Proper hurts. But I keep goin, switch from a fist to a palm, fist to a palm.

Iqra It is my job to bandage them once they have been stitched up. I work quickly. Starting from their thighs, I unravel the bandage and wrap it round seven, eight times until I reach their knees. I wrap the bandage twice at their knee and then carry on down four times, until I reach the ankles. I put a blanket over them to keep them warm, so they do not go into shock. I talk to them, tell them how brave they are, tell them how proud of them we all are. Tell them they are now women. The small ones I can carry by myself. Carefully. I try to make sure the blanket covers all around them so the other girls do not see the blood. But sometimes they bleed so much you can do nothing to hide it all.

Muna Some woman opens the door an' I don't take the time or trouble to tell her who I am. I rush straight past her, an' I can smell that smell of antiseptic an' blood again. Smell it like it was only yesterday it was me the one bein cut. Smells putrid in here.

There's people in the livin room, women in the livin room, but I don't pay no mind to them, don't even look at them.

I head to the room where I smelt that stink seepin from under the door an' I burst in. I see her. I see her an' my heart sinks. I'm filled with emptiness. See her holdin down some girl like a scene from a horror movie, blood all on the floor, blood got all on her an' the elder. She's dressed like she thinks she's a nurse or summat, a medical assistant.

Proper dressed up for the part, proper clinical. She stops an' looks at me in shock. Elder stops too. This is real. They're cuttin little girls in a tower block on a Saturday mornin. Like they do this every Saturday mornin. Like it's nothin.

She looks at me like . . . I dunno, like she's lost. Like she's let me down. Like she needs me. I look back at her like she makes me sick.

Look down at the mattress. Feel fear an' relief at the same time. The girl layin down bein mutilated, sliced apart . . . she ain't my sister.

Iqra I let go of her legs and my hands start to tremble. I see her mouth wide open, but I do not hear the screams. They are drowned out by the pulse beating hard in my head. Muna, my friend, stands before me and I cannot concentrate. I cannot focus. She stands as if waiting for an answer or an explanation, but my throat is dry and I have no words.

Muna The smell's all up in my head, but I tell myself I ain't gonna pass out in front of her again. Ain't about to fall into no unconsciousness. So I try an' keep calm and steady.

Iqra 'Muna.'

Muna She calls out my name like me an' her are friends. Don't know who this girl is. Me an' her will never be friends. Tell her I wanna know where my sister is. Elder stands there eyeballin me. I stand an' eyeball her back. Blood drippin from her razor like she's turned butcher man. She says my name again like she ain't sure it's me standin in front of her.

Iqra 'Muna.'

Muna 'This is how you spend your weekends, is it?'

'Keepin up tradition?'

'Gettin 'em while they're young?'

'Where's my sister? I swear, Iqra, if you've touched my sister . . .'

Tries to utter some explainin but stumbles. Too shook to make any sense an' I'm too incensed to stand here an' listen. So I get movin. Fling open the door to the other bedroom. Nothin there. Jus two limp-lookin mattresses lyin on the floor. I'm about to peak, 'bout to reach my eruption if I don't find her. Go back into the room with all the chairs. The three of them follow me into the livin room – Iqra, the elder, and that smell, only now it's fresh blood that's makin me wanna retch.

An' that sickness stays with me in my pit as I make my way past the waitin women, get to the back of the room an' see two of them lyin there, tiny bandaged bodies like casualties of war.

An' all it takes is a second, jus a second, for my heart to be absolutely shattered into a thousand pieces.

Iqra She is next to her. Kneeling. Crying. It reminds me of when my mother found Hdafur and wouldn't leave his side. She stayed there with him like that until they came to take the body away.

Muna Feels like a battle's jus happened. Feels like war jus took place on her body.

Iqra I took part. I gave a bullet to the soldier to shoot. I've given that soldier a hundred bullets and watched her shoot.

Muna I remember that feelin she's feelin. Shock. They think splashin a bit of antiseptic down there an' tyin some flimsy bandage round you is gonna make it all better. All will be fine. But it won't be better, it won't ever be fine. 'Cause eight years on an' I still ain't fine, far from it. Wettin the bed at fifteen 'cause my own body's out of my control don't make me fine. An' all these complications make it complicated for me to get help 'cause doctor's gonna ask why I'm closed up, not opened up like other girls, why I'm left with jus a tiny hole. Gonna want me to talk about it, speak out about it, an' maybe I should. Maybe I should. 'Cause none of this is fine.

An' she's lyin there. My little sister. She's lyin there on some stranger's floor in her blood-soaked dress.

Iqra We do it because we have always done it.

Muna Lyin there like some messed-up Sleeping Beauty.

Iqra I do it because I am expected to do it.

Muna Like some broken rag doll.

Iqra Everything will be okay now.

Muna Looking far from a princess.

Iqra Everything is okay now because she is clean.

Muna She's just a frightened little girl.

Iqra Her husband will be happy she is pure.

Muna She's seven years old.

Iqra A good Muslim girl.

Muna She's seven years old.

Iqra   I look down at the blue-and-green sweet wrappers, and I notice how the blood has soaked into the cracks in my hand, like tiny rivers.

Muna   Blood that's flowed from her is makin streams on the floor.

Iqra   We do it because this is what we know, it is what her daughter will know, and her daughter after that.

Muna   She's seven years old.

Iqra   We do it because . . .

Muna   (*singing*) 'Happy birthday to you –'

Iqra   Because . . .

Muna   (*singing*) 'Happy birthday to you –'

Iqra   Because . . .

Muna   She's seven years old today.

(*Singing.*) 'Happy birthday dear Leyla, happy birthday to you.'

The End.